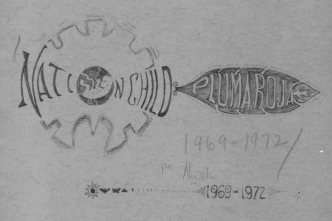

NATIONCHILD PLUMAROJA

1969-1972

1969-1972

Published by Toltecas en Aztlan
Centro Cultural de la Raza
San Diego, California 92101
Phone 235-6135 or 235-6136

811

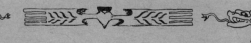

Toltecas en Aztlán Publications

Technical Editor y dibujo   Víctor Orozco Ochoa

Copy Editor   María Moreno

Illustration   Esteban Villa
Armando Núñez

... dedicated to Human Truth (Social, Economic, Political,
Historical, and Ecological) and Chicano Harmony which in
our belief can only be practiced through Mutual Self-Respect,
Self-Determination in our endeavors and the Self-Sacrifice of our
individual differences for the sake of a Centro Cultural de La
Raza where our indigenous ancestral spirit of brotherhood and
sisterhood, justice and peace can flourish in contemporary
Chicano art forms...

● ●

the red Spirit of Aztlán: a plan of National Liberation

in the Spirit of a new people that is conscious not only of
its proud historical heritage, but also of the brutal yankee
invasion of our territories, we, the chicano inhabitants and
guardians of our motherland Aztlán, from whence came our fore-
fathers, reclaiming the land of their birth and consecrating the
determination of our people of the sun, declare that the call
of our blood is our power, our responsibility, and our inevitable
destiny.

we are free and sovereign to determine those tasks which
are justly called forth by our house, our land, the sweat of our
brows and by our hearts. Aztlán belongs to the Creator who
brings nourishment to the seeds, and brings rain and sun to the
fields to give people crops for food, and not to yankee empire.
we do not recognize capricious borders on the Red Continent.

brotherhood and sisterhood unites us, and love for our
brothers and sisters makes us a rising people whose sun has
come and who struggles against the allien yankee who exploits our
riches and destroys our culture. with our hearts in our hands
and our roots in the soil, we declare the independence of our Red
Mestizo Nation. we are a Red People with a Red Culture. before
the world, before all of northamerikka, before our brothers and
sisters in Amerindia, we are a Nation, we are a Union of Free
Pueblos, we are Aztlán.

end the genocide and biocide
    of the yankee empire
            humanize
            conscience
            organize
    for National Chicano Liberation
            build
            a
            Red Nation

ooÞ

Victorozcacha

o o o o

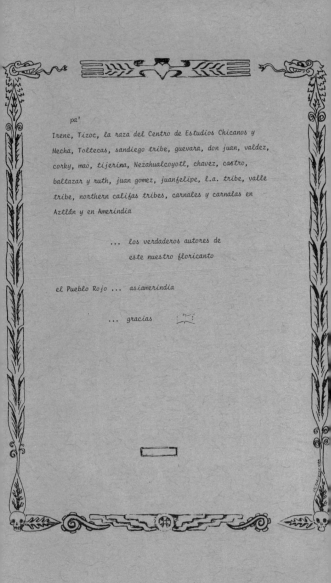

pa'

Irene, Tizoc, la raza del Centro de Estudios Chicanos y
Mecha, Toltecas, sandiego tribe, guevara, don juan, valdez,
corky, mao, tijerina, Nezahualcoyotl, chavez, castro,
baltazar y ruth, juan gomez, juanfelipe, l.a. tribe, valle
tribe, northern califas tribes, carnales y carnalas en
Aztlán y en Amerindia

... los verdaderos autores de
este nuestro floricanto

el Pueblo Rojo ... asiamerindia

... gracias

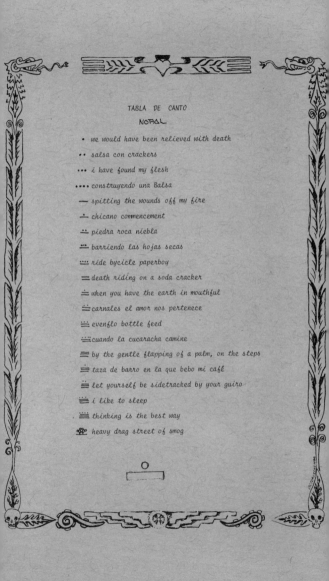

TABLA DE CANTO

NOPAL

- • we would have been relieved with death
- •• salsa con crackers
- ••• i have found my flesh
- •••• construyendo una Balsa
- — spitting the wounds off my fire
- ÷ chicano commencement
- ÷ piedra roca niebla
- ÷ barriendo las hojas secas
- ÷ ride bycicle paperboy
- ≡ death riding on a soda cracker
- ≐ when you have the earth in mouthful
- ≡ carnales el amor nos pertenece
- ≡ evenflo bottle feed
- ≡ cuando la cucaracha camine
- ≡ by the gentle flapping of a palm, on the steps
- ≡ taza de barro en la que bebo mi café
- ≡ let yourself be sidetracked by your guiro
- ≡ i like to sleep
- ≡ thinking is the best way
- ❀ heavy drag street of smog

O

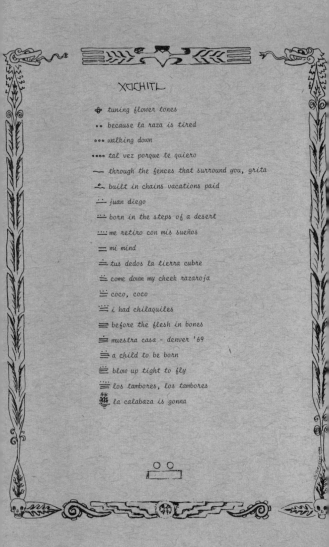

XOCHITL

- tuning flower tones
- because la raza is tired
- walking down
- tal vez porque te quiero
- through the fences that surround you, grita
- built in chains vacations paid
- juan diego
- born in the steps of a desert
- me retiro con mis sueños
- mi mind
- tus dedos la tierra cubre
- come down my cheek razaroja
- coco, coco
- i had chilaquiles
- before the flesh in bones
- nuestra casa - denver '69
- a child to be born
- blow up tight to fly
- los tambores, los tambores
- la calabaza is gonna

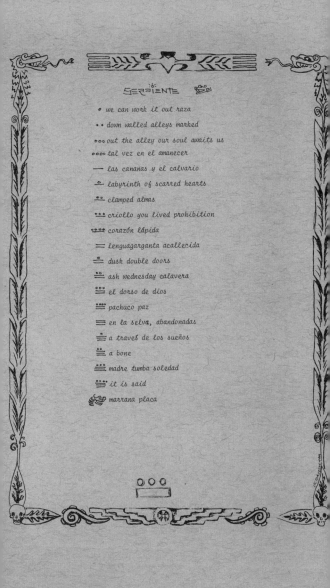

SERPIENTE

- • we can work it out raza
- •• down walled alleys marked
- •••• out the alley our soul awaits us
- •••• tal vez en el amanecer
- — las cananas y el calvario
- ≘ labyrinth of scarred hearts
- •• clamped almas
- ••• criollo you lived prohibition
- •••• corazón lápida
- ═ lenguagarganta acallecida
- ≛ dusk double doors
- ≛ ash wednesday calavera
- ⸪ el dorso de dios
- ⸬ pachuco paz
- ≡ en la selva, abandonadas
- ≞ a través de los sueños
- ≣ a bone
- ≣ madre tumba soledad
- ≝ it is said
- marrana placa

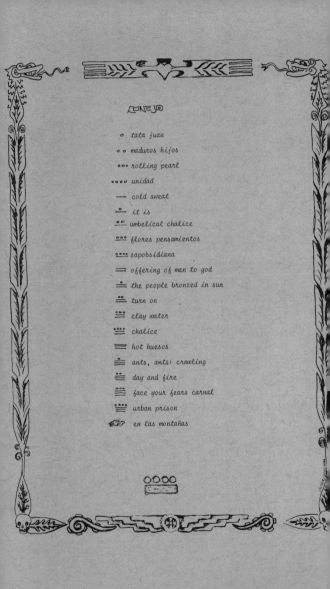

CONEJO

o   tata juan
oo   maduros hijos
ooo rolling pearl
oooo unidad
— cold sweat
it is
umbelical chalice
flores pensamientos
sapobsidiana
offering of man to god
the people bronzed in sun
turn on
clay water
chalice
hot huesos
ants, ants: crawling
day and fire
face your fears carnal
urban prison
en las montañas

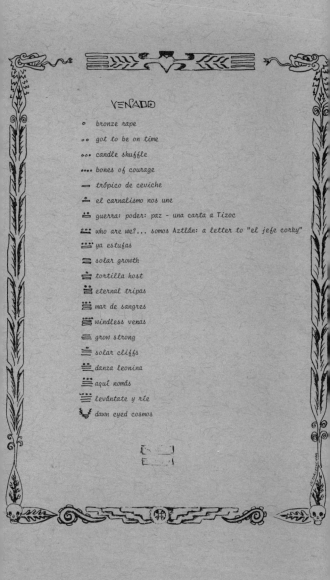

VENADO

○ bronze rape

○○ got to be on time

○○○ candle shuffle

•••• bones of courage

━ trópico de ceviche

⁎ el carnalismo nos une

☰ guerra: poder: paz - una carta a Tízoc

☷ who are we?... somos Aztlán: a letter to "el jefe corky"

ya estufas

solar growth

tortilla host

eternal tripas

mar de sangres

windless venas

grow strong

solar cliffs

danza leonina

aquí nomás

levántate y ríe

dawn eyed cosmos

"Once a man has vanquished fear, he is free from it for the
rest of his life because, instead of fear, he has acquired
clarity- a clarity of mind which erases fear. By then
a man knows his desires, he knows how to satisfy those
desires. He can anticipate the new steps of learning,
and a sharp clarity surrounds everything. The man
feels that nothing is concealed.... It gives him the
assurance he can do anything he pleases, for he sees
clearly into everything. And he is courageous because
he is clear and he stops at nothing because he is clear.
But all that is a mistake; it is like something incomplete.
If the man yields to this make believe power, he has
succumbed to his second enemy and will fumble with learning.
He will rush when he should be patient, or he will be
patient when he should rush."

Don Juan, from The Teachings

WE WOULD HAVE BEEN RELIEVED WITH DEATH

we would have been relieved with death

       i know

en el sillón espero el pelo blanco

           de seda rapping

             to me lips labios rojos

en guitarra corrida de arena en llamas

       if burnt; carne quemada (chicharrón)

relief

     tal vez cansado de esperar

        sin sueño

i will dream again

        satisfecho, relajado en mí papel

para encontrarlo

gratis and live

even if relieved,

          i would have been

sin carrera, sin apresurarme

         a la muerte

no iré a mi entierro

    my epitaph will be blank in my solace

SALSA KON CRACKERS

salsa con crackers

cómo? con la boca

prelogical fruit

    prehistorical experience entre las palmas

entrando a preprimaria

y a la salida

    after school con chona

a las quesadillas

    de la bruja con limones embotellados

and cucumbers con chile piquín

-a veces jícama

a veces nada -sin dinero without friends

pobre and abandoned; hungry

crackers do not quench my pangs

    my gut

swelled

tengo hambre

      crackers do not show their fangs

no bite, no poison or enchantment

sin sabor o nutrimiento

even con salsa

    arid, dry, desiertas de calor

☼ ☼

I HAVE FOUND
MY FLESH

where is the oasis where one heavy lays his mind
to the frescura del arroyo tierno placidly flowing,
such a rose bud would sprouting en el centro del
desierto sin circunferencia more often than not i've
interrogated myself? to discover, compounded with a
multitude of textured answers, sin encontrar respuesta
alguna he decidido no preguntar, dejar mi pasión por
el entendimiento y descubrir que ante the vaccum which
the lack of action originates caos nace en el orden,
la secuencia.

i do not know why or stand under that which already
is, por lo menos en la imaginación de algunas gentes,
and consequently find myself at the commencement of something to be that has terminated su asociación con aquello
que alguna vez fue. having such been the finished pro-
duct chiseled by the artistry of my will habiendo deseado
voluntariosamente vagar en el laberinto del libre albe-
drió encuéntrome viviendo.

henceforth i can only do but that which the assertion
of my self implies in the form of a must. little less
puede resultar ante al encuentro accidental con la muerte

forging the skeleton of its structure into a mobile
having conquered time in its cooperation with fixating
space i can only cry or die; however i, being one never
to mind my mind, have chosen the exception to my mind-
ing it. i suffer y estoy vivo en el acto de mi afecto
por la muerte.

    tan cerca como el sol .

        la muerte acecha y brilla en mi balcón

    triste ilusión eterna la que me fija

    anchored to my toil

        me muevo con las olas

    azoto las rocas con mi pecho

standing under moonful of bones

i could die naked

derretido sobre cobble stones

a media calle

ante su semblante rostro emaciado

    i have found my flesh alive

en el recuerdo pestilente de su presencia

i live, i love

i cry in the desert aliviado

CONSTRUYENDO-UNA BALSA

perhaps one day, in the angry thrust of my dreams,
i will discover la verdad en la mentira que me
rodea. at the pinnacle of my climb clouds episode
in sequence to that which once was, i will eat mis
tacos con salsa without fearing a colibri to come
and suck mi miel i will go to misa, to the church
where to the saints we light velas. and we know nothing
nor do i see any more stars than those assigned to me
by light years and space bondage.

in view of such arid limitations pretendo convertir
mis sueños en los que me encuentro ante el aroma que
mi piel despide evaporating now, to rain mole tomorrow.
it is then no surprise or misguided expectation that
materializes itself in the form of calavera romántica
que cena con la muerte, tortilla en mano and entirely
committed to the act of being. what, as an obstacle, goal
or inclination to discover of seems quite irrelevant in
view of the how, within which my behavior is implicit.
el estilo y la manera en que mi forma se desenvuelve
undergoing metamorphosis in amphibious terrains es,
entonces, el medio primordial

�֎ ✷ ✷ ✷

en que el palpitar de mis venas sufre ante la danza
y los manjares de chilimaíz que brotan de la
mesa and for my hunger.

   de tal manera que mi ira resultará inevitable-
mente como la tarde que llora ante la presencia de
la luna y de la noche que se avecina. no more
to bear the burden on the shoulders put my mind
away para que nadie meta el codo en aquel
mole.

   o en salsa de cera
   en comida veladoras nunca
la cocina de barro y de frijoles pintos
manchados en la herida, melting
construyendo una balsa
(la travesía es difícil)
death in ambush eats tortillas
chilaquiles con queso
   y vino de maguey con tunas
our prayers to be electric
         to be plugged and light lunas
ante los santos soles
   los de rifle y cananas, los de hueso

SPITTING THE WOUNDS OFF MY FIRE

spitting the wounds off my fire

    i cried

grite en el ocaso de la tarde

    cuya capa de nubes me cubre y arde

"among the nations

    as it is among individuals

respect for the rights of others

      is peace"

benito juarez came to mind

bienestar social le llaman

    limosnas que ciegan

en mi mano de polvo y lodo nunca

la dignidad terciopelo verde

    suave y acariciante

      ante el roze de mi piel

dignity in my being chicano

      demands respect

en mi fé yance mi error

    mi fé en el conocimiento terzo

i failed to understand the lack of

    in him from whom

i once demanded (dignity unknown)

CHICANO COMMENCEMENT

chicano commencement

        exercising freedom, breathing

        in zapata's gown

            i found myself graduating

me encontré en el comienzo

    en el origen-principio

de mi raza-creciente

        en lágrimas ante el techo de mi choza

tata chente, gonzález, pancho cervantes

reunidos

    furia en pecho pancho saize

issy chávez, irma castro

      todos juntos en el rezo

a nuestra raza la misa

a beginning seed of end to sorrow

    self pity and quiet never; when

the boil is on

      up tight today

      loose winds, caress mountains

tequila y salsa con tortillas

    de maíz

    nace apenas in our tassel

PIEDRA ROCA NIEBLA

piedra roca niebla

heavy lid of waterfalls on burnt cheeks

ojos rojos de coraje en plumas de Quetzal

fixated mound of moonful

    of dreams frustrated leaps

    dripping faucet bleeding thirst

i in the pond sink never

ranas desiertas en flores de pantano

derramando sinfonías en el velo luna noche

piedra roca

    niebla piedra roca

    piedra niebla

    roca piedra (pesada azucena de dolor)

tengo sed

mejillas misteriosas medusas

caballeros tigres montañas de voluntad

chanting in the dusk cavern of sensuous pebbles

stones

    precious tears aged in sulphur

rock

    rhythmic arrows bathed in war paint

fog festival of rising red struggle (sink never)

BARRIENDO LAS HOJAS SECAS

barriendo las hojas secas

      rastrillo en mano de pizca

la casa en ruinas de sueños de baranda

climbing fences ivy covered huts (dogs barking)

wire walls transparent dividers

    away, away - lejos de mis brazos

mi mano no alcanza y mi escoba no barre

    no barre el polvo

        las hojas

    el dolor y la pobreza llora rocas

lavando las ventanas de cartón en el verano

sulphur afternoons wind glooms -- hair flows dark

negros ojos

    negra suerte en el jardín de yerbas

weeds in solitude thrusting isolation saturdays

    wooden webs for fences fragile (spiders in the grass)

mowed lawn of dusty cans cardboard and nails

"buenas tardes"

    buenas!?

    buenas pa' que!

       pa' nada!

pa' barrer, pa' respirar, pa' soñar (en hojas secas)

☆☆☆

RIDE BYCICLE PAPERBOY

ride bycicle paperboy
                    juanita on handle bars hanging
clinging to raspado dreams
ride, ride
                    kitchen hungry child
tortillas y frijoles velas de esperanza
feed juanita - sell the papers, ride
naciste pá pedalear
                    jorge neverstare
neverstare at the sunrise of your doom
doom you may find in outhouse
paint the planks
                    ride in the absent laceration gone
to madera vieja
                    splintered afternoon set fire
if only the ice of your raspado
                    turn your dreams to miel
feed juanita
                    ride your oike
sell your paper
                    burn your outhouse
paint the walls and have an ice cone

never jorge child stare

at the sunrise of your doom (pull the shades

                    find the sunset on the water

                         melting to begin)

to build a bycicle

            to ride

    your own

to swim

        raspado sweat on chest

con valor (el tuyo)

            vigila las calles - ride

y el bienestar de tu raza

                de la especie

(la humana) opuesta solo a la muerte

dedicada a tierra fértil

        no para explotar

only to reap fruit

            earth's tribute to humankind (ness)

maybe

            vigila, guarda tu suerte

guarda el destino en tus manos

        ride

DEATH RIDING ON A SODA CRACKER

death riding on a soda cracker

    hassling badges and clubs at hand

        to crack skulls

  to crack walls

      to crack death on adobe halls

    man, don't know the hassle of his badge

            the clubing kill

      or he don't know what's living

he don't know, no sabe nada

           absolutamente nada

vacío su pecho de emociones rosas rojas

      verdes realidades

no sabe nada

    the man, he cannot see carnales

carnales de pedernal

    en la paja de este mundo

      una chispa prende el fuego

light up chicano bato

    enciéndase sola carnala y encienda

    encienda la paja

on the comal get our tortillas going

feed our children con frijoles

                con la sangre of our fuego

a los niños, nuestros hijos alimenta

traeles to our mundo nuevo

           al mundo de raza fuego

           donde chicanos descubren realidades

en verdades de ternura

           la revolución desnúda

in the open thrust of platitudes

        of reactionary attitudes

        of apathy, avergonzada

riding on a soda cracker

          blindness in helmeted skull

sucia muerte negro y blanco, colorblind

         colorculture blind

se ha olvidado de su vida

        to remember goldcoingod

le ha prendido veladoras a su dios

dios, moneda; oro y plata pisoteante

WHEN YOU HAVE THE EARTH IN MOUTHFUL

when you have the earth in mouthful
        to chew con los dientes de esperanza
        un sueño de pueblos rojos
how can anyone misplace barro
        el barro de la gente en notas
            (musicales) tardes de espera
        y espera, y espera
        sin que el sol se acueste, no
aparece el dolor lunar en carnes
        y el barro no se cuece
como un sueño en la mano
            chicanos do not loose sueños
        y de sí son propios dueños
        chicanos, mechicano dreams
y los sueños que acozan durante la comida
are the same dreams that facilmente
find the opening cavern to the labyrinth of
chains. chains are fallen. decrepit find
the bunk in cell. slept on the beach
for a while. lights on, guards pacing
cannot find the recovery of
sleep. and cannot wait for the crepuscle.

cannot loose the dream for chicanos shall
loose ourselves. and of ourselves we are
masters. chicano masters of chicano
sueños de color frijoles con salsa y con
cebolla. dentro de la campana que
repica hidalgo - fuera de la iglesia
el padre clama justicia, libertad y
tierra. dentro de ella nunca existió
dicho sueño - no pa'l pueblo, no pa'la
raza, pa' la gente; pa' nosotros
nada. "ni ma' carnal" me dice
el bato; "se acabo la onda." i don't
understand that kind of payasadas.
con mi gente no se juega. a mis
niños no le quita nadie los frijoles.
se acabo la espera mr. jones,
"señor" jones (perdone uste "patrón").
i don't care if you call yourself my uncle
and remind me that you ain't my
dad. my dad? mi padre era
zapata, juarez y madero mis
hermanos corky el león, chavez

el palomo, y los berets they are my
brothers. mis carnales son chicanos.
mis carnales son humanos mr. jones.
and the relativity of your coin
makes you meaningless. to me to all
who call themselves i, and assert
su sangre y su valor de cuero, de
hueso colorado. you are meaningless
mr. jones. and tell your vieja mrs.
robinson - your ex-wife frigid man!
that we ain't falling for sus faldas ni
cortejos. our barro digs on warmth and
you mr. jones are a frigidair of pestilence.

     an ice joke on your martini
     cubical skull you got
     we weep and in lakes round flow
     y our raza se baña en arroyos
     donde cantan las ranas con guitarras
     y los grillos hacen el falsete
     we got our razared
        we got our barro
     we don't need your "holy" breath

CARNALES EL AMOR NOS PERTENECE

carnales el amor nos pertenece

raza bronze no perece

en este clima no muere

nos pertenecen las calles, el barrio

the phone posts and electric bulbs

the mailboxes are ours to use

in the afternoon a letter send

to other chicanos, with blood seal it

settle the foggy paper into flight

free the spatious lines

empty of figures, write

write to your carnales

let them know la pachanga's on

on today for all

pa' todos to feel alright

pa' lo que queran frijoles

pa' los que queran cañones

there will be a flying bird in the sky

to sit down and cry by

y pa' los que queran liberta'

there will be tequila raza

con sal y limón

EVENFLO BOTHE FEED

evenflo bottle feed
    to any child
water boiled drink
    no milk give
rocking in the craddle
    of his birth
pa' soñar bonito
    pos' aquí ajüera
ta' muy feo
metido en la botella el barco
    without breeze of water
        sail to sea, to shore
a la orilla del rio
        donde el bosque se espesa
soup of sulphur and oxide hopes
there in the bottle
    el cerdo de la bureaucracu
devora the entrails of his skull
    inside out color
a shadow surplusultranill
dispensable sombra de botella
    comercial mamadera cristal

CUANDO LA CUCARACHA CAMINE

cuando la cucaracha camine

en our libertad crucificada

on the wooden planks petrified statues

on the nail a cross beneath a man

we will know the sound

the bells of our impatience gone, by

waterfallen sounds of solitude to joy

i was then a little altar boy, kneeling

while the cucaracha crawled

muddling through the crumbs the cucaracha

crawled, and crawled; dragging her soul

not knowing bread to be abundant she lagged

and went hungry

pangs and clamor

to be heard in the dusk of a

morning dew

chicano mass

to preach about the kingdom of man and woman

(god has been ruler long enough as god)

men and women have to learn themselves about

one another, to love each other

(chicanos will then preach of the kingdom of god)

BY THE GENTLE FLAPPING OF A PALM, ON THE STEPS . . .

by the gentle flapping of a palm, on the steps
    outside sitting, i find a lot of injustice inside
my arms wrapped around in the winter
neck up turned (built-in scarf)
    my bones freeze before the frigid pig
lacking of warm blood turned bluebadge man
    of white to serve,
        the retrograd status quo
not the people, white workers, disillusioned youth
black souls
    not chicano hearts, or red or yellow
skins, not the east not buddha
        (the lover of mankind)
not any warm blooded mammalian
    the pig a hog leg in his holster
frigid armature, poor imitation of homo sapiens
and the breeze shatters my eye lids
    half closed in desperation to be blind
ugliness wants us to run away
    let your blood boil, it's been frozen
get inside of yourself carnal
    get your fire

TAZA DE BARRO EN LA QUE BEBO MI CAFE

taza de barro en la que bebo mi café

   humo pendiente de mis labios se evapora

there is time still in the water falls of anger

chicanos en el barrio

      esperanza en cancerosa célula

      en el capitalismo radica la moneda

en el socialismo viven los hombres y las mujeres

      viven como pueblo entre hermanos y hermanas

no como zombies cuerpos

entre robots traga monedas

   carga pistola y maze

               helmeted skulls

   to serve you unto death

in capitalism there _is_ a choice

   we can die poisoned by decrepit,

   anachronic socio-political institutions,

   (we can die slowly)

or we can die quickly

   massacred in our cry for justice

LET YOURSELF BE SIDETRACKED BY YOUR GUIRO

let yourself be sidetracked by your guiro

carnal let yourself be free

to do your music when your heart pounds

in the melody of your ringing ears

unto death do not allow your love to pass

unto life embrace other carnales

help each other sweat the day away

eat your tortillas together

carnales we gotta share our joys

in the Quetzal pride

on the pyramid of sun glaze birth

get together

make your music

make your canto raza

make your barrios

make your lives carnales

make la raza live

unto life juntos

  bajo el sol de nuestros padres

I LIKE TO SLEEP

"i like to sleep
        with a lot of sarapes on me, man"
"i like to have heavy
        dreams of sarape colors, bato"
we hear and fail
        to listen or even understand
we find ourselves in a shell
        of corporation, military nightmares
of success, of co in

                co opt

                cut out

                        sp

                                lit

                                        go

                                                n

                                                        e

y el bato likes heavy dreams
        and doesn't turn on to smog
he don't like coinshells
        he knows, la vida
no vale nada sin tierra
                sin libertad

THINKING IS THE BEST WAY

thinking is the best way

        to travel by the clouds

        and sink in flower tones

        in foam flourescent sands

to travel in free associations

todos juntos, nosotros

ya no va haber pedo carnal

        ahora clickeamos juntos

la raza is together bato

        it ain't never gonna break

esta raza no se quebra carnal

'cause we gonna think it out

        together, juntos

in one thought la razaroja

        can be told al mundo

a todo el mundo, juntos we will

        discuss, argue

        and disagree

        and find new ondas

ondas on which we can find

        a new nosotros

        a raza nueva

HEAVY DRAG
STRET OF SMOG

heavy drag street of smog

shadowed shelter of adobe blocks

i am reminded of

carnala

     la raza es de bronce

de piel sedosas carnes

en las que descubro la cascada de pelo

          que te acaricia

          que te da calor

descubro a margarita

        entre las flores aroma de barrio

        de ternura tarde

        tarde, cansado de esperar

i find no time for fighting other chicanos

i can only hate in them

     what i lack in myself, la raza's proud

carnala

     la raza es de bronce

finding my way in the fog

a butterfly

a dream

a choza pa' descansar la cabeza

TUNING FLOWER TONES

tuning flower tones
　　　　guitarra sings in serenata
the twanging, twanging, tone
　　　　　　to tablas tuned
the thumping of a rhythm shoe
tapping, tapping, taconeo
y el latido de la sangre
en el corazón explota
las burbujas del sol
el de Cuahutémoc, Tizoc
o el plumado Moctezuma
el sol de la tierra
the plantation pains
and pangs of hungry lives
trabajando en la cosecha
today, we live in the waste pockets
　　　　　of the city wild barrios
batos locos en protesta social
　　　　caminando en clickas
together in the dusk of orgullo
humming hums of slow paced tunes
seeking peace

BECAUSE LA RAZA IS TIRED

because la raza is tired

i find time in molasses thick

we cannot wait

      because la raza is tired

we cannot wait

the moving red sun is out

          to shine a crystal dream

to walk an autumn leaf to earthy drought

to bring water in cubetas

         put out fire of red uniform

arriving to feed on ashes

en las ruinas calaveras rocas

     tristes recuerdos vacios of a dead people

genocide, genocide

we cannot wait, because

wait because la raza

tired, torn we cannot wait

while la raza's being born

WALKING DOWN

walking down
    abajo, abajo hacia el cristiano
    suelo de licor, de vinos
    de uvas aplastadas gentes
la raza
    walking down church yard road
epitaph written in confessionary box
    ready to be buried
nunca
    las campanas del pueblo
    repicando afuera pa' que el campesino
    pa' que el campesino la oiga
el entierro de la gente
    bajo árida tierra
    seca cosecha, sin maíz
    arroz o frijoles
walking down
    down the christian licorice floor
    de aníz y de azucenas
    incienso y bosque
bosque de pinos occidentales

TAL VEZ PORQUE TE QUIERO

tal vez porque te quiero

    raza mía

molted bronze unto a god

    chicano-hermano, hermana chicana

derretido en las llamas

    razasol

because i kneel before you

weeping in my hunger's joy

caring not for nothing cold

    but the people razared

de calor que en borbotones nace

calienta los frijoles, el arroz

        y las tortillas

perhaps that's why i love you

       razared

        rojaraza

   razamía

tal vez porque

   vez porque te quiero

porque te quiero

   te quiero todavía

razamía

"THROUGH THE FENCES THAT SURROUD YOU, GRITA"...

through the fences that surround you, grita

yell through your heart clamored hope

dreams be crystalized in the struggle of today

a gritar - con el ardor de la sangre

> viva la raza! que viva!

> que viva, pa' siempre

si tu alma llora es porque la muerte

la calavera te acecha, mas lucha, lucha

la muerte en azufre espera

carnal, tu tropiezo añora

mas no, nunca!

carga tu pistola en mano y grita

> viva la raza! que viva!

porque la raza es de bronce!

> de barro nuestras facciones

> y de oro son nuestros sones

> canta carnal

> grita y canta por la raza

que la revolución truene

> que nosotros venceremos, venceremos

venceremos

BUILT-IN CHAINS
VACATIONS PAID

built-in chains vacations paid

    social security

    and retirement soon to come (in velvet)

barf the opium idiot box zombies eat

machine bolts

    attached and riveted, en la cruz

    agonizantes and apathetic

placing bets

    rooting teams and clamoring

    blood

que se vea sangre!

    sangre! sangre de color ... no blanca!

    sangre muerta pulsa en sus alambres

la máquina se envenena

    and stupefied zombi men

sterilized, homogenized

    objective as a victom of its object

    itself the target

    of a broken dream, in yesterday's rain

excreted on the pavement, concrete wall

run over by its own wheels, gears blind

vacations paid (redeemable when dead).

JUAN DIEGO

juan diego

chicano hermano

revolucionaria raza

vision de villa

en la madre

morena frente rojiza

nosotros !

todos nosotros

in motion

pendulum swing en el cielo

carnal !

carnal, sabes que ?

lo que pasa

es que

       i'm basically happy

aunque mi general villa

quera llevarse al amor

la mesedora

la mujer del movimiento

la soldadera colorada

BORN IN THE STEPS OF A DESERT

born in the steps of a desert

on the sand a lagartija

lizzard thirst that of our raza

acostumbrados al hambre

nos damos cuenta en la sangre

en la muerte

    rojas tardes esperanzas

de dolor y de agonía

la raza sufre y conoce

    la raza knows much of back pain

    of working, sweating and dying

así, así raza

comprendamos el desierto

y con agua

quench our sueños

quench the throats that thirst for water

drink to live today, mañana

mañana y ayer are instants

today, ahorita

la lluvia

la de truenos

la de gotas y relámpagos

riega mi jardín entero

ME RETIRO CON MIS SUEÑOS

me retiro con mis sueños

con las plumas de guerrero

con el hacha de Tizoc

    el artista, el hechicero

plumas ... feathers on the forehead

clay ... barro en los dedos

annointed raza de fuego

burning and yelling and living

to die someday in the struggle

la revolución, la raza

gente, gente roja

con historia

con presente corazón en mano

gente, people, raza

    willing and in fire consuming

entre mis sueños y el fuego

    poco es el frío de mis huesos

sun glazed in our sweat

    the struggle

la revolución, la raza

la de plumas de guerrero rojo fuego

MI MIND

mi mind

    constipated with tortillas

    is found to be with joy, con alegría

    y con salsa colorada piel

    de bronze

    sedabrown

a people glazed in barro

flying to the pyramids where the sun strolls

casting shadows of sorrowful wounds

lacerations casted racist fever

el menjorge de mago

    -hechicero chicano

    -frijol grabado en la frente

heals, alivia cold calenturas

con sangre pulsante

    -hirviendo en la muchedumbre

la raza

a people born in the struggle

la lucha

la luna llena

    -las tortillas de mi sol

la libertad, la nuestra

TUS DEDOS LA TIERRA CUBRE

tus dedos la tierra cubre

la raza vive en la tierra

sembrada la tierra es nuestra

labrada, llorada (en sangre sudada)

frente en alto vibra bronce

venerando al sol moreno

-calor que corre en las venas

valor que vive en los hechos

en la choza de la gente

encuentro en comal frijoles

las tortillas sudan fuego

y la salsa llora sangre

encuentro la raza nueva

la que con la mar se acoje

la que con la tierra duerme

en las raíces almohadas

en las palmeras los sueños

en los sueños brotan llamas

en la vida arde la carne

  suda la revolución

  la raza late, y se impone

  y la sangre es derramada

COME DOWN MY CHEEK RAZA ROJA

come down my cheek raza roja

to caress mis pómulos salientes

    -i want to kiss the mejilla that adorns

    bronce brocado

tu boca exhaling el espíritu de la sangre

nuestra sangre

    boiling in the backyard

thrust into the open callejones

cactus field of rocks and polvo

    y tierra húmeda

in our macetas

a semilla

    a possible nacimiento

raza!

raza! !

    take the time to be born

take time by the neck

    turn it into an arado

    cultivate el maíz de nuestra

identidad indígena

    a la vida, a la muerte

al nacimiento de un nopal

Coco, Coco

coco, coco basin headed programed man

        pistoled mouthed

        shotgun carrier to protect

hassle, hassle plated badge recorded tape

        que te lleva, que te agarra

        que te come; ya me dice la mama

"se llevaron al padre

        al hermano

        y al tata le colgaron de su orgullo en un papel"

coco, coco

    vienes coco, sin caballo

    sin estribos y sin silla

coco, coco

    vienes coco ya montado

      ya pegado a tus botones

      con tus máquinas de hiel

coco eras tú, coco, coco

    de orgánica manera

      ya el miedo, ya la sed

      pero ahora; we don't know you

mounted, riding on conveyor belt

inorganic... coco, coco basin headed death and frigid breat

I HAD CHILAQUILES

i had chilaquiles
    salsa joy and onion fire to pretend
        deafness to tambores   thirsting
                              gasping
                              begging
i had chilaquiles
        to share in ollas de color-pintadas jarras
        white man dug our spice and shun our breath
        he came to us to eat
                and ran
                and ran in his forgetfulness
of us, of our salsa de colores (yace dios)
        en el pan de los abuelos
        in the clamor of their toil
            sembrando maiz
        slapping tortillas on their palms
a shape is born
        to tear and mingle in tomates
to burn and weep in chile verde
            o colorado
to be the universo of our hunger's vision
i heard tortillas boil, and maiz was broken

BEFORE THE FLESH
IN BONES

before the flesh in bones

took shape and dialogued

in the breakfast of tortillas

blind to los cielos y la tierra,

we were a wooden image,

a projection of the dioses que le hablaban

molcajetes volaron en protesta

atrapados entre una opresión enjuta de madera

y un destino de cadenas y promesas

de salsas que elaboran sentimientos

(lacking then in us)

la sangre carecía de alberge

and the rivers of blood no circulaban

porque? porque..? que tenía que pasar? quien habría de morir?

porque no hablaba con los dioses

este cuerpo de madera

había de ser quemado.

they who crawl and fly al fuego se lanzaron

la serpiente emplumada se hizo sol y el cascabel...

el cascabel en víbora prendido

comenzó la música que hizo al pueblo de fuego.

NUESTRA CASA DENVER '69

cuetes de malinches lenguas

    preocupied statues

    piedras entumidas, sin calor

      y sin amor moreno

el carnalismo nace como la tuna

    entre espinas de dulzura

    el color sarape de contrastes

y la marcha

    la marcha-mestiza

    sentimientos que flotan en el aire - la bandera

razaroja praying to the sun marchando en la misa

    power to las manos que trabajan

    power to all who dig tortillas

y que se bañan en sudor salado

    trabajando en penitencia

      haciendo liberación

piernas waking to the marcha of our pueblo

our gente, en los barrios

    en las escuelas

    en las canerias

    en la pizca

    en la calle (our steps are measured)

chale! we can't take no measurement ... chale!

no more rezos de rodillas

no more apologies por ser de carne

　　　y de hueso

porque tenemos hambre and our children

　　　are singing con orgullo

the children are just beginning to be people

　　los pueblos ya espinados are hungry

　　　hungry for tunas

　　　　for dulzura

　　　　por amor de carnales

nuestra casa es nuestra casa

　　　tenemos que laborar juntos

　　　tenemos que organizar the disarray left

　　by he, the master of cadenas of oppression

　　　tenemos que construir de adobecorazón

　　　　a casacalor de fuego libertad

nuestra raza es nuestra raza

　　　and the tunas of our struggle

<u>are</u>　eaten en nuestra casa.

　　　fuera muebles coloniales

　　　we gonna sleep with sarapes

to dream our sueños de fuego

to wake el espíritu que vibra

     en la sangre que nuestra razaroja

               ya llora,

                   ya clama justicia

¿ dos caras we've been born

nuestra madre, mujer india-asiática

nuestro padre el europeo-africano

         nuestro corazón mestizo

      has now grown bigotes, brochas y hasta pelos

con el frijol en la frente,

with cheekbones facing el sol encuerado

         drilling freedom in the clouds

la bandera Mexicana kissed the heights

         kissed corazones

        y entre gritos el espíritu moreno

thrusting flechas in the statuas

        tongues once forked are silent

   quiet ante la verdad morena

that our suns have calentado

casa raza, razaraza, carnalrojo

ríe, canta risk your life for la causa

        live for la revolución que nace ya en nuestra casa

A CHILD TO BE BORN

a child to be born

pregnant is the continente

el barro y la raza

to bear Aztlán on our forehead

el niño que como pájaro

en su vuelo de colores cantos

guió a Tenoch hacia el águila

el niño dentro del vientre semilla

una madretierraroja le acaricia

Aztlán, Aztlán of the continent that bears child

tu madre es - el continentetierraroja

where the crickets call the birth

and the ranas arrullan al nacido

y las víboras del mar siguen a la campanita

por donde pueden pasar los de adelante

and the ones in the back se quedarán

Aztlán, Aztlán

the semilla que plantó nuestro padre Quetzalcoatl

ya germina

en el vientre de nuestra

madrecontinentetierra, Amerindia

nationchild de su padrecarnalismo Kukulcán

BLOW UP TIGHT TO FLY

blow up tight to fly

    in the nubes of our joy

raza never die

    mujer eterna raza

raza nueva, raza raza

in the sarapes find the truth

en los colores contrastes de tu piel

razaroja, razablack,

        up tight

today, in the swamps of pestilence

heavy dreams on our shoulders

an open redpath to follow

libres, al fin

razalibre

razanace

razaroja

fly in up-tight blow

LOS TAMBORES, LOS TAMBORES

los tambores, los tambores

tocan, tocan

en la puerta raza

tocan, tocan

open the wounds of your heart

to the sun, to the sun

burn, burn raza

mientras los tambores

tocan, tocan

corazón ama

llora y vive

corazón

LA CALABAZA IS GONNA

la calabaza is gonna

       turn into a car

to drive in midnight abrelatas

for all types of latas

an opening opportunity dark

in the dusk of a pumpkin

such are dreams

sueños pesados de esperanza

la realidad de frijoles hierve,

el adobe ya aparece

to wake

in crimson dawns

and wet sidewalks

and fog

and stench

dark dusk slipper

lost in a half night

WE CAN WORK IT OUT
- RAZA -

we can work it out raza
our troubles mutual
over a plate of frijoles
we'll have tortillas be warmed
and live together
la raza junta
chicanos free from cold cubicles
la raza nueva
while the owl mediates cactus dreams
la raza marches on with machetes
a la selva pizca siembra
pa' construir la nueva raza tradición
to smoke peace out of a love pipe pasto
sheep grazing on cheeks, while
sitting en la junta raza nueva
trouble conflict chingaderas
we can work
    can work
        work them out
to remain juntos

DOWN WALLED
ALLEYS MARKED

down walled alleys marked

    "el grifo de la logan"

      con la tradición del "qui aui ri qui"

el gallo anciano sabio

el patriarca de la logan

de los callejones

entre los garages

detrás de la tortillería

bajo el poste

con la raza meets

in the birth of a night

discovering the flicker of dawn

sun of pyramids

sun of suns to grow red

fire beams and warmth

kicking a can full of buts, split

walk

    down marked

    walled alleys

callejones de cartón y lata

OUT THE ALLEY
OUR SOUL AWAITS US

out the alley our soul awaits us

to meet on pebbled streets the breeze

the bongo rhythm of our thumping heart

to catch the wind the odor and the flesh

to launch our gaze on once lost hopes

a candle

sitting in lonely stare

a tear

irrigating our cheekbone high lands

pyramids, feathers and rituals of love

people in the dusk afternoon of a cloudy horizon

love

Quetzalcoatl in life rejoices

and we walk down age carved alleys

running to find alma, sangre y aliento

feathers in stomach gnaw melancholiac ulcers

and Huitzilopochtli drinks our blood

raza rain in Tlaloc's agony

raza run to the sun and sing

of the barrio

and the soft winds that flagellate our skeleton

TAL VEZ EN EL AMANECER

tal vez en el amanecer

la nieve de tu sangre en agua se convierte

fría realidad, fea sombra

disappear

your welcome is over, genocide

go hunt yourself in suicide

people eat tortillas

while the rooster of the cannery

the whistle blows, the silence of a

morning breaks

and the máquina camina

con el sudor de la raza

el aceite en las aceras

leaves fallen during a lost season

another year

another page to fill, a can of beer

such is the want of a máquina

a chicano takes a siesta only in

    the meditation of our struggle

    in the consecration of our people red

    raza

    tal vez en el amanecer

LAS CANANAS Y
EL CALVARIO

las cananas y el calvario

dos hermanos en su muerte

    bullets seven shot and planted

      tear, tear bullet

que yo te veo en mi machete

      ignored you will find yourself

    calvario, penitencia

te desea mi flagelado cuerpo

    parado en el corazón

    rock of solitude

        now

    burning ~

our penitence de rodillas

      nunca encontrará la muerte

el carnaval de dolor y las máscaras de cristo

    brutalized facades in hiding

all masks be fallen, be flown

    al rugido de una flecha

las cananas en el barrio

      la liberación calvario

"mejor muerto y bien parado

than beg living de rodillas"

LABYRINTH OF SCARRED HEARTS

labyrinth of scarred hearts
    wounded in the sown struggle
    sproutings in the making of a
        historical leaf of radical movement
a people powered in red clad faith
en penitencia guerrera
en revolución morena grasp
    serene hands on the earth
plowing, plowing
    watering in tears for torn backs
and burning perspiration in the fields
a few paths lead, follow and walk
      alone, to the light out the cueva
out the solitude caverna de miedo
on
to the path that has a heart
a nomad drinking agua de barro
cortando la maleza
    con machete voluntad, cutting the earth
healing the wounds planting barro
      planting paths with heart
        and clarity

CLAMPED ALMAS

clamping las almas de un pueblo
de nuestra gente que vibra
cuya cola cascabel, cascabelea
rattle, rattlecoil
let the clamored hope to breathe, ...
breathe!
en el pecho de Aztlán
-el soplo de dios Quetzal
-culebra tierra de barro
tear the brazos off the máquina
off with its mediatized head
let the tuercas gorge and splatter
for el corazón is mourning
where spades are called machetes
donde las armas son cuetes
ruido verdad y guitarras
let the last alambre burn and breath be rattled

CRIOLLO YOU LIVED PROHIBITION

criollo you lived prohibition

                    tras la cerca del ibero

la colonia tu tortilla

                    tu techo, the meztizo's agonia

          tus jardines el sudor de aquel vendido

          and your plantations of thievery

          encueradas al sol testimony

                    con espigas y maiz

la cosecha de un pueblo robaste

          y robas vestido aún ahora

          y´violas la manta y te llamas chicano

          y chupas la sangre del barrio

          y te dicen batman - yankee sacón!

face your color, face your face

                    and then mírame a los ojos

                    parejo si te atreves

a sudar conmigo en las tareas de la tierra

CORAZÓN LAPIDA

on the history of our wounds

the epitaph of our hearts pounds

to a cuerpo de carne

roja sangre tocapuertas, toca

el alma

el espíritu que cascabeleando vuela

vibramuerte a través de un evil - eye

o una aguja marker en la carne

of a tierra arrebatada

where the lápida of our flesh

shall caress the stolen land

and kiss the rocas, a mother

indiamuerte en plumas,

y en cananas

junto a la tumba, la madre!

our sangre, la resurección morena

LENGUAGARGANTA
ACALLECIDA

lenguagarganta acallecida en seco ardor,

in the fire picazón that boils a breath.

la carne de los labios brama.

    the palabras that mutiny a tongue

        crave to be spilt en llamas

        to splatter paredes arrugadas

        upon which silence falls;

    and the rooftops of tongues

        crawl in flight to the cuevas

        in prayers de rodillas laceradas

        pesadillas y recuerdos fried in chile

gritan, our tongues gritan el derecho

              gritan justicia;

and the forked ones encadenan

        en azúcares drogadas

twist our culture y envenenan

and the fire picazón boils en alientos

rapes melcocha mouths

      to feed them lava

burning con chile la lengua

      and the lies del arrastrado

DUSK DOUBLE DOORS

dusk double doors
   dirty cadenas of odio
   chained to the sweat shops
            the sweat fields and prisons
(outhouse omens)
open dawns of cold rushing,
rising in calvary thorns
freezing the spines of our pueblo
         nunca !! el colorado pueblo
         never !! nunca ...
in our barrio occupation is not allowed
let the barrio
      be a barrio, barrio, barrio.
barrio and not blood sweating colonia
planting cactus flower pots
regando el jardín de plumas
salute the sun in ayunas
mis labradores,
      carnales ... tear
      open las puertas de Aztlán
      fuera del fil y de espinas
a proteger nuestras flores.

ASH WEDNESDAY CALAVERA

ash wednesday calavera

where the warrior eagles stand

   on the forehead

               no more ashes

      to grey dust

               no more our flight

      to the solar god of war

               death incarnate

   Huitzilopochtli

cheek bones torn

worn down flesh

      once forgotten in the dusk

      staring from the dark

alone

      a thrusting truth of tripas

      flocked together

      bursting into birth

baptized with the thunder of cuetes

      in the spiral

(meditation-of a will to be)

alive

      to kneel before la raza

(burning flesh)

      and be blessed

in the death of eagled ash

EL DORSO DE DIOS

in the trepidous flight of a bird
    Quetzalcoatl gave birth to its death
en las rocas
    las nubes morenas de su rojo sol
deslizáronse en agua
      miel y rojapiel
coloring its wool into skin
hicieron temblar los zenotes
    y los pueblos
y en las rocas quedó la emoción
    --el carnal de la cuatro
      perdió su dolor
  por dinero cambió su color
    color miedo de lunas
    cambió
    por un sol
  y en el dorso de dios
    el águila perched
    sobre isla y nopal
    víbora devoró
in the fall of a bird
    Quetzalcoatl gave birth to its death

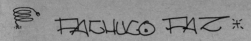

PACHUCO PAZ *

we can all reach the point

    of knowing ourselves

        to be Mexicans in the north

Mexican air with placas on walls

      names to be found

or carvings be read

      leaving no tracks

or marcas in the wind

music is born

      and la fiesta del silencio

permeates our hearts

and our blodd pounds a beat

      to reach the point

where and when, rhythmically

      we know ourselves

to be

        chicanos de colorada piel

        de espíritu guerrero

hunting in our own land

      nuestra tierra

EN LA SELVA, ABANDONADAS

en la selva, abandonadas

putrid tunas asoleadas call

gritan, gimen y se quejan

del calor y de las nubes

waiting for the worms y lagartijas

sobre los nopales rojos

the stench settles in the wounded

the stench settles in the fog

y la soledad regresa al nido

el perdido encuentra su desierto

and the clouds bring shades and pensive shadows

las heridas de la tarde se desangran

in a pestilent effort to be healed

agonizantes ante las flechas del sol

llorando por la luna

una

tuna

se pudre

A TRAVES DE LOS SUEÑOS

a través de los sueños

entre las necesidades de la carne

bajo los violados soles

i found a calpulli

warm tortilla plates of broken spears were served

    the palmeras staring at the windy passion of their storm

and the children running naked en el callejón

    everybody was there y el espíritu de la

música

música, música

      sica sica musi

música de sarapes, de contrastes

    de cuetes y de cananas

en la sangre de mi raza rojapiel

Δ BONE

a bone

time

it shines with

a bone in one

hand

strange fate

dusty dreams

of immortality

of power

omnipotent

dellusions

last waves

rippled waters

trickling blood

hemorrage

and death

killing time

it shines with

a bone

in one hand

MADRE TUMBA
~SOLEDAD~

madre tumba soledad

    the fluttering of wings breathe papalotes

Papalotl Papalotl al sol ya vuelas

    on the string terreno que te jala

papalote encuentra tu razón destino

climb your cola de colores to the sun

skip the postes, slide

glide, Papalotl, Papalotl

      (gulp a crumb of leaven bread)

en tortillas calentadas serve your soul

bite the dusty bones of war and breath

    (break tortillas en tu comunión)

cut the venas of our blood and share

    crack abrazos and bring rain

where the tips of fingers touch

    and·hearts are caressed in clouds

   where roofs de palma bring shade

los dátiles de ilusión crumble

sueños tighten bolts and drive harsh nails

    to devour las tripas of the wind

    lápidas rise

    to the sun of quiet epitaphs.

it is said

it is said

             that Motecuhzoma Ilhuicamina

sent***********

         an expedition

looking for the northern

            mythical land

wherefrom the Aztecs came

         la tierra

            de

            Aztlán

         mythical land for those

         who dream of roses and

swallow thorns

         or for those who swallow thorns

     in powdered milk

feeling guilty about smelling flowers

         about looking for Aztlán

RAZA

MARRANA PLACA

revolution rape to mutate pigs

in the exasperated pangs of empty stomachs

kill for love of an angered freedom late to come

kill in yourself the oxide of your pestilent fear

assassination crawl to pigs and to those

                              running naked and afraid

mutant supper of aromatic exposure to the sun

like it is

tell yourself no lies, but sour truths

and sulphur boil for blood have for your nectar

mañana the thirst of drought and lacerated solitude

may swim along with you in death wish water falls

today, in the desperation of your cry sore throat

arid dreams can find oasis with nopales wet

razared be born to the cavern

to the obscurity, to the blackdark stench

razared be born

after your suicide mutation birth to quench

to the caverns bring a river crystal bath

to cleanse a pig

to rape a fear

to strip a lie and tell it like it is

in the desert of your sweat

the wetness of a tear add a bit of salsa

warm your plate

and of bones rid of en la libertad alada

fly with anchored heart to kiss an earth worm in his plight

razared be born in lungfull suck of dew

on fertle ground plow freedom

in the volition of your flesh

eat the frijoles off the palm trees in your islandgreen

partake of your bread

razablack, white, razared eat together

let the stare of pig grow blank

bland isolation he has reaped to die (alone perhaps)

the volution of our libertad has cried ya basta

to restore el pan de cada día

the pig will have to join our linda nación

to feed jorge, margarita, who hunger libertad

SUN

TATA JUAN

if you see tata juan
con joroba caminando
speaking good english
    kind and careful
      and methodic
shuffling his body like a mountain
      rock of hope-now
          and tomorrow gone
jorobado se quedó
      ante los botones de su destrucción
playing with a máquina
      revisiting his childbirth
or working on his epitaph
    carving his tomb into tatooed cross
crucificado en la joroba de su jale
say to him
    carnal tu corazón palpita liberación
    respeto y hermandad humana
deja tu máquina chicano hermano!
    deja tu joroba y endereza tu vida
      tu cultura y tu razón de ser
caballero águila
    seguidor de las garras
      de la mano de bronce

if you see tata juan

dile que dios no es de lata, de fierro

ni de aluminio

dile que dios es de bronce

que guadalupe es Tonantzín

y que san pedro es chicano.

MADUROS HIJOS

la carnala y la carrera de san juan
en el anochecer de dudas y de miedos
san diego con sus rosas reza
guadalupe la madre, mujer-raza
madre de maduros hijos
pechos de rojizas carnes
corre, corre carnala
for we will grasp your palm
to stay, to live with us, mujer morena

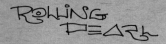

ROLLING PEARL

in your eyes the sparkle of a dream

in vain

in solitude

you flow to seashore mother pearl

perhaps the winter of your moon gloom

wet to drip

to melt and bathe in pebbled paths

will find the strolling of a cricket lost

in symphony to cry, to crawl away

to die but laugh

and laughter fill the freshness of your lips

your flesh to warm

embrace perchance the void

the chasm of your cry

the clamor and the blood to burst

explosive butterfly to fly

in the host sand and foam splash

your freedom find and hope

to walk again

the tracks that you have inscribed

to pass

to walk again your shadow cast

to tear the housing shell of tears

ᗡᗝᗡ

and find yourself to be

          a rolling pearl

on blades of grass before the sun, a light

    the cavern of a gasping call

      in darkness never find your flesh again

but in the self of you a taste of loneliness

      an aromatic flight to kiss

a rib tide and a quiet stream

your smile

UN CAFECITO

UNIDAD

       estamos juntos, unidos al grado que participamos

en cada una y otras vidas

en las vidas de cada otro

en las vidas de otro cada

en cada otra y unas vidas

en cada sol unidos in the darkness of

       our light

en cada soul juntos in the struggle of

       our national liberation

       together

   to the degree

   that we may participate

   in each others' lives

nosotros estamos juntos

   estamos unidos

pero no estados unidos

   el poder yace

   en el pueblo

   y no el estado

en nuestras manos la unión

en nuestras manos la junta.

pa' celebrar la ocasión

nos encontramos unidos

es decir, juntos

es decir

    estamos unidos

porque la tierra

es pa' todos

y no na' mas pa'l estado yankee

COLD SWEAT

de vez en cuando
la realidad del papel
ante mis ojos cristal
en el dolor de mis palabras
descubro cavernas de oscuras sombras
sueños de madurez en rocas
rocas rojas
rejas tardes en la carcel del ser
nunca, siempre
acaso la importancia del ser
calavera seca en el desierto
desesperadamente
lloro, por dentro espinas
arden las carnes
y la realidad se huye
le pierdo en el sueño
en la esperanzada fruta
en la ya amargada tarde
se precipita el sol
y la mar hierve de frio

it is

it is in the fundamental and ultimate interest
of our people,
of the people that would care to join our marcha
of an agrupation of red people that can
envision a concrete reality, and direct
resultant of our dreams to be brothers and sisters
in the blood.
and in the spirit
    that binds us to this earth
and to the death that we can all
foresee as: inevitable decomposition
of our personalities as beings
of individual choice
of personal dedication to our claims
of this tierra
    as the one where our origins walked
    as people in society that have toiled
    as people in culture that have gathered
    as people in a human dwelling
across the bridge of time and legacy
Aztlán is our tierra
    our nación
    our dwelling
    our responsibilty.

we are not just being occupied
we are being allowed to survive
        under an illusion
an illusion that heavy on our eyelids
        believes in the omnipotent paternalism
of an angel sent from heaven
        to liberate us from the european oppressors
and establish the self determination
        of a continent that, from its inception
was casted in bronze
        and not in clay or ribs.
sickly we believe that the machinery
        through which we have to be
processed and departmentalized
is one that is parallel
            if not better
to the natural historical
            developments of the seeds of
the ones that have sweat blood
            on this land for milleniums
la máquina es un anacronismo
the bolts that bind it were
            not casted for our protection
or security but for

for our safe keeping-out-of-the-main-stream
        mainstream of melted
elements to bathe no longer europe
        but the biggest white settlement
in Amerindia, northamerikkka
el espíritu de liberación
        the spirit that thrusts us
                to seek an opening, gasping
        for breath
shall inevitably be casted
        in respect for human dignity
and in due dedication to
        the nationalization of a land
where the rich shall cast off
the jewels off their masks
and pledge psychologically, spiritually
        and materially the surplus
        of our toil to build
having chosen not to destroy
        the system which will bring
our people forth
                to be secured in employment
purpose and meaning in
        our historical calvary to the

liberation of our feet
            of our hands
            of our hearts
            of our minds
        and most important of all
                    our fervent spirit to be
before the implacable machete
            de la muerte de los pueblos
that has presently infected the societal
                organs that oil the creaking
            socio-economic artifact of yankee society
and those who live under the influence
            clicking clumsily in the world of
                make-believe
            and close their-eyes-real-tight
                pa'arremedar a los yankees
what the hell for?

UMBELICAL·CHALICE

the umbelical chord of my dreams
craves the marcha que mis padres engendraron
in the chalice that
once held
to be truly a pachanga
el padre nuestro y guadalupe
and the blood of the holy chalice
the time has come
for all good men
to come to the aid of their country
and to the misa de colores carnes
simon que sí
que me prendan veladoras
que le digan a don juan
que no permita el día
when i, blind
fail to come
to mis carnales
to find the origins
the roots
the seeds
and the tears shed in the struggle
to remain
the jardineros of our destiny
to the soil, la madre tierra

in the vientre

  thimble, needle, cloth

thread doth?????????????

  do you dare carnal?

do you dare fall off the teatro

  the deception where máscaras are worn

and facades are painted every day to sell

  themselves

or the articles of their commerce

or the spirit of their blood

  the time has gone ·

      for all the space

  has not arrived

      for all evil persons

the itch

the witch

the ditch

  they all got together and you know what?

do you know what?

do you know what?

do you know what?   no?????????????????????

      well ....

      .... i don't either

because it was a bruja

      y la comezón de mi alma

that brewed the womb of ages

        where the men of barro melted into soil

and the monos de madera burned the sun con plumas

        where the man of carne y hueso

     traveled through by blood and brotherhood

     bearing a child of a witch

     itching to be in the ditch

      where the white witches once itched

la magia del corazón

      germinó en el espíritu

      germinó en el bronce

      y en el pueblo

in the umbelical dreams of my soul

FLORES · PENSAMIENTOS

thoughts in words
                    speak flowers
on the lips of men
                    who pace time
to the disciplined pounding
                    of a heart.
songs strengthen the path
                    of he who has listened
to the wind tunnels that spray
                    the lungs of love
                    that blossoms truth
                    naked before the sun.
tearing the walls that secure us
to a world of our imagination
                    the bird sways the thought
the wind and the night hover gloomy
                    in their joy

SAPOBSIDIANA

sapos de obsidiana plague dreams
　　　and ametralladoras
aim sharp
　　　and shoot solitude
　　　in our pelos we can feel
the tremor and the blood
which many red people
have tried
　　　to drink
eyes in a taza de barro
in a plato de arroz
　　　como hongos feed on
the ashes of thought persued
　　　and dreamt again
con la ayuda de un sapobsidiana
　　　de severa cara
　　　　　smiling

ｏｏｏｏ

OFFERING OF MAN TO GOD

offering of man to god

    unwind

    unwind

    unwind the chord

the binding breath of earth

    of our umbelical history

    unwind

    unwind

    unwind the mind

that triggered shuts to kill

    and rape the path, bleeding

heart gasping into wilderness and sand

    a sun to see burn our fears away

    and bake our faith

    unwind

    unwind

    unwind your heart

into a trunk that offers music to the spirit

    and the woman of red flowers

offers melodies that trickle

    upwards to the flat topped pair of wings

that flap, flap, flap, flying to

the cloudy pillows of a dream

    of winds that wind

    around and upwards

    to the sun

THE PEOPLE BRONZED
IN SUN

i'd be

    done, gone

razared, a long way a head

pero si nos vamos juntos

    venceremos el miedo y el abuso

we'll be long gone

we'll belong, gone our fears

    and the tear fertilizers of dreams

razared, i'd be done

    gone to my head the moon

when we want to reach to sun

    (el origen de nuestras quemaduras)

gone the sun

    orphan skins

would seek a father, a mother

    would seek the reason of our flesh

and the destiny of our

    fearless

hearts daring abuse

to the people bronzed in sun

TURN ON

turn on
to your selves
'cause, carnales, carnalas
there just ain't
no carga
or righteous droga
as the self
that our heart bathes.
in blood rinsing
you can have
her strength
in you be shown.
slow down
look at your self
married to the bronze
that profiles our cheekbones
rising to the redsun's caress
and to the struggle of temples
in our breathing selves.

CLAY WATER

clay water

pulsating paths of pebbled rock

ages bygone of flesh

       molten   molten

    effigies flowing   in arterial mountain

ribs broken in angered flight of weaponed hand

         an ally

         an ally

           object of power's search for dwelling

           lost to the pyramids

gasping blinded yellow

        the sun and its daughter

          tierra, tierra

          continente

          contingent of dreams

               of feathered heads

          and songs of blasting silence

red thirst

    breathing blood esse

    bending backs or flexing chests

    breathing blood esse

barro breath

    dust jar of painted smiles

CHALICE

in the sceptered chalice

    the womb of solitude

and the blossoms of beating

    hearts, pounding - at once

in a path joined

    por la música sangrada

    en la muerte de miedos

juan persigue nubes

and skulls that spit

    births on palms opened to

offer flores

    "juan ...

        juan diego, corre

    derrama tu carne

        look at Tonantzín

    en el monte de pétalos

te ofrece sus rosas

    la madre morena

en cáliz de bronce

HOT HUESOS

hot huesos

and war pending

    on the tearing of a jaw

chewing tripas

    pledging to the sun

a victory of hearts

    and fluids run

    down mejillas

y pómulos salientes

    guerreros en combate

madre tierra

    yield

    yield

    yield the fruit of

    ages

    maíz

    maíz

tripas gush in caldo

bones crack open

    guerra

    guerra

    grab, grab

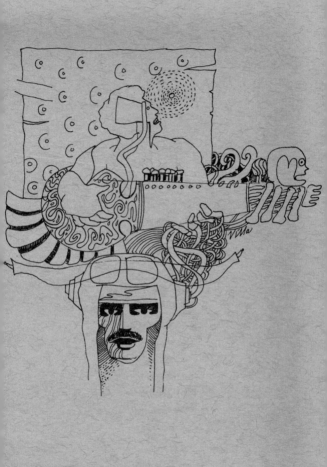

bones of hunger war
        split heads
                and corazones
offer, pledge
        no more
        no more
blood cooked in oil
        veins plugged in grease
grease
grease
grease the gears
        machine bolts running
hearts bethroded
        married to the click
clack, clinging to the jaws
        suicidal grab
grab, grab a bone carnal
carnala grab a bone
and watch the warrior die.

ANTS, ANTS; CRAWLING

anthills climb through corridors
    run upward to the crater of the mound
    run downward to the heart of burning soil
corridors and labyrinths of heat
    sun rays flashing
    creeping spiders dead and gone
      carried, carried
ants of crumbful backs
and queens sit tight for flight
    to bear in womb
    more ants
and queens lay eggs to sacrifice
      and bake their wings
the sun, the heat and corridors
of angered crowds
    gathering dust, clamoring
      more, more
peace razared peace
    but when to see ourselves
now here, now gone
      in anthill climb
to find no thing
    no crumb, no heart,

what for the rush and bloody boil
        and pounding, pounding
clicking to our pace
        our selves now gone to hills
            in craters
                    cracks and lonely darkness
        not a light
a step to follow gone to free
            ourselves to come
and bring forth backward
        thrust of death and ugly
scars
        the earth yawns
while cave mouths chew away
and tremors fill our veins
            with gasping lostness
windy flight to burn
            and come again
to give birth bleeding
        sunbaked carcasses
in fat bellied
            hungry, thrifty
        crawling, craving,
            climbing ants.

DAY AND FIRE

except those that crawl and fly were sacrificed

it was their custom to converse

    with their own hearts but

the wizards sought to snare him, Quetzalcoatl

so that he would offer human sacrifices

symbols of his omnipresence were the

        other gods and not dead men

himself the scriptures and the wisdom

the plumage of a bird that rends

      itself; men are alive

"humanize their desires

    fortify their hearts

recieve a strict instruction"

    tlamantinime

Cáhuitl (that which is about to leave us)

like the night and the wind

is now here to stay in the day and in the fire

FACE YOUR FEARS
≋ CARNAL ≋

do not ask of the sun

    to give no light

or ask the moon to hide

    her skirt of stars

do not torment your hearts

    and tear your faces

learn to live

    with the darkness

    with the wind

face your fears

die only once

    or a thousand times hiding

your face

    covering your ears

from the daring songs of your

    heart

hearten your pace into darkness

learn to live without

    asking your god

to be kind, gentle

    and to change; you walk

the moon will sing brighter

    in her skirt of stars and open your ears

the sun will color your heart and open your eyes

URBAN PRISON

la gorda de aluminum foil

arroz with corn and chícharos

    on top

presidio hill

    where the honchos

       on top

         rule

      the time has come for all

      good men to come to the

      aid of their nation

and the ones

    on bottom in Aztlán

struggle to breathe freedom

only to find

    the bondage of the slave

in the skies covered

    with clotting blood clouds

of smog bars and

    dark chains of

factories smoking death

and coughing life in spasms.

En Las Montañas

up the down ward
    slope of valles
and cañadas
    where rivers caress
      the cheekbones of our meadows
and the sun comes
      in ayunas mañanas
bañadas in mist
    breathing water
falling to the ground
and maiz reaching for
    the skies
we took peregrinaje
    to the madre
sierra de montañas
    con pinos
y bellotas, a veces
ardillas y carpas
refugio we found in
    cuevas
pueblo indians nos
    declan
while our doors opened
    a little to see the pale envy of the yankee.

BRONZE RAPE ✿

la india se arrodillaba
    en el río,
a recoger agua iba.
    mujer de fibra.
bronce tez; apenas
       notables the round
    moons of her breasts
and hair dark; flowing
    to the breath and
will of Ehecatl padre
    del viento;
y de la aventura alada
que prendió al criollo.
    en su bronzeada caída
kissed her forehead
    and raped the silence
of the trickle, trickle
of the stream
    pulling the ground
to her red plumaje screaming
el mestizo
    ante el altar
nació sin padre
    pero sí con mucha madre

· ⅅⅅ

GOT TO BE ON TIME

time carnal time

got to be

on time mounted

riding yourself unto years

of aging bronze

piel growing, rippening

bursting into softened

silken bronzed

gold skin fathered

by the sun

aging now into arrugas

turning la

rueda de la vejez

and time

carnal, time, time

clicking hours

pounding unto death

piercing silence

piercing ears with time

bound to

time, redbrother

time long gone

time short coming

time been walking dead

the time has come
    to come
    to come
to the aid of our nation
    Aztlán
    Aztlán
land of sometime
    aftertime
noontime, notime
    afternoontime, suntime
alltime
nighttime, moontime
    morning time,
have atole con pan
    dulce y gordas
con queso y salsa
    sometime land
of our time and age
of the fifth sun
    darkened
with the smog of
yankee rhythm machines of time decaying

CANDLE SHUFFLE

shuffling wax on

    the pavement protest

of a vigil walk

    on bishop's cathedral sleep

raza froze with

    candles in hand

and fire in our hearts

    whose cries died

in the thick blanketry

    of the constipated sesos

in the bishop's calavera

we walked and talked

    and sang and

    argued but it was

palm trees and the skirt

    of starry darkness

that savored our plight

    pidiendo posada

en el nombre

    del cielo

esta encapotado and so

    is el obispo

buenas son las nubes

    pa' la lluvia

bueno es el obispo

ᘓ ᘓ ᘓ

pa' regar la sopa dreaming
    while we hold
    a velorio
to come into and share
his dreams
or to celebrate
    his abdicated death
covered in black robe
    con cruz
pendiente al ombligo
    carga la
crucificiōn en la panza llena
de sermones about
heavenly kingdoms for
    the working poor
who are meek
    and give thite
"10% pa'l señor!"
    cual señor?
el señor sacerdote!
la señora iglesia!
"el cielo!! el cielo!!
that never gave us posada

BONES OF COURAGE

the bones of courage

are with the máquinas

the máquinas that bore

the child of death

hiroshima

hiroshima

hiroshima

the human máquinas

from

the

laboratory created genocide weapons

to protect their fragile

loneliness

their allienated minds

lost

without bodies

sin corazón

que marque sus veredas

walking theories

afraid to experience

to learn with their bodies

to breathe

to pace our progress

with the beating of our heart

ᘒᘒ ᘒᘒ ᘒᘒ ᘒᘒ

pumping courage to our
　　　　　　work
allienated minds
　　　　of walking theories
　　　　need to be awakened
　　　　torn from their dreams
　　　　and thrown
　　　　into their bodies
　　to rot in flesh
　　　　or learn
　　　　to bear the
　　　　　day and night
　　　　that crawls and flies
　　　　in the womb
　　　　　of
　　　　mother tierra
　　　　　　tierra
　　　　　　tierra
　　　　　　tierra
　　　　　　tierra
　　　　　　Amerindia
　　　　　　Amerindia
　　　　call forth the sun
　　　　　que suba el sol
　　　　　que suba el sol
　　　　　que suba el sol
　　　　　que baje

después

la oscura capa de estrellas

después

la luna

y la noche de vientos

y cantos

y sueños.

que suba la luna

que bañe la tierra

que perfume el vientre

de la tierra nuestra

Amerindia

Amerindia

Amerindia

deja ya que crescan

deja ya que brillen

tus hijos

que brillen los hombres

en la oscura muerte

del alado miedo

padre de hiroshima

que muera

que muera la máquina-muerte

en los huesos

que muera en los huesos

y que brille el hombre

el hombre de Amerindia

la mujer de Amerindia

los hijos de Amerindia

           Amerindia

           Amerindia

las hijas de Amerindia

           Amerindia

           Amerindia

tierra de bronce

mestiza tierra

mestizos pueblos

           Amerindia

           Amerindia

           Amerindia

TROPICO DE CEVICHE

a los orígenes de coco y palma

donde sentada espera

en su altar

the morning star

guaymas de tierra mojada

buenos días

sol

viajemos juntos

hawks sweep

clouds of desert dusk

mochis, mochis

m-sixteen dad

    Mexican soldiers

profanely sink

their g i botas

on Yaqui ground...

no has llegado

a tus aniguas raices, MÉxico

te añoran tus nopales

en tus madres sierras frías

and windy nights

sing by

against the yerbas

plucking melodies

from puntas de maguey

Yaqui winds.

carve epitaphs with polvo

on antiguas rocas

y jacinto dice

"pacensia raza,

pacensia"

chavalitos, children

roll to sleep on petates

by el fuego

covered by our lady's

skirt of stars

and surrounded by painted

desert darkness

the silence of the cactus

sings

no has llegado, México

a tus antiguas raíces...

"policía militar

patrulla Mazatlán y todo

centro urbano,"

estudiantes explican,

"intrusión del pulpo yankee

estrangula

tierra y libertad

indígena"
tentacled yankee octopus
arms pri's army
así
la milicia Mexicana
mantiene cuchillo al cuello
Tepic, Nayarit
ojos de dios ·
te acozan en las montañas
Huicholes, Huicholes
in manta pants,
huaraches and rainbow colors
sarapes acinturados
y campanas al sombrero
ringing paths of rhythmic melodies
Huicholes y Coras
offer their hearts
every day
to our father
sol con plumas
and our mother
tierra faldepalma
ya jalisco deja oler sus
tierras rojas
mojadas plantas callejeras
descalzas, sobre calles empedradas

la raza en Tuxpan anda

cruzando el rio san pedro

pa' la feria en rosamoranda

pasos suaves encaminan

tropicales alientos y sonrisas francas

murmuran, rosamorada

amorada rosa

pacíficas aguas

las faldas tropicales

uncover their coconut breasts

fresh water

rich oil for ageless

skin

la raza mama

la chichi e coco

y se protege del padre del tiempo

no has llegado

a tus antiguas raices, México

you are not from here

and you are not from there

you have no age

you have no future

you are not thirsty

nor is there any water

go back

go forth

rasca la tierra

busca el sol

everyplace, everytime

    lord and lady of the close vicinity

    navel of earth

    circle of fire

river waters

ocean waters

       mis maloya

       mismá loya

mismaló ya

    mismaloyá

sá lamandra mis maloya

salá mandra mismá loya

salamán dra mismaló ya

salamandrá mismaloyá

salamandra de los montes

mismaloya de los arcos

you have no age

you have no future

you are not hungry

nor is there any corn

     regresa

rasca la tierra

toca el cielo

busca el sol

EL CARNALISMO NOS UNE;
INDIO JUNIO SEIS

el carnalismo nos une
    y el amor hacia nuestros hermanos y hermanas
nos hace un pueblo ascendiente
la carne nos une
    en sufrimiento
    en dolor
en gozo, en alegría
los golpes y las caricias
los gritos y las sonrisas;
raza, raza, raza, raza
la pirámide de nuestro espíritu.
las raíces de nuestro corazón
    en las caras de los niños
nos recuerda la pureza destruida
    por la muerte ambulante
del yankee sin corazón
      sin dirección
      sin vereda
la vereda que nosotros, como pueblo, atravesamos
se ha encontrado con espinas y con tunas
    con monstruos metódicos y eficientes
con cárceles, con ejércitos

con fábricas y con minas

con campos y con escuelas

donde reina el silencio programado

por la máquina asesina

que idolatra a un dios verde, de papel

que compra cuerpos

pa' trabajar en los campos, fábricas y minas

pa' hacer guerra en Amerindia, Asia y África

pa' traer la misma muerte y dolor

que nos aqueja

a las puertas del hogar en que habitamos...

muerte, muerte al perro de papel!

el monstruo que le creo

se atraganta con el sudor

con la carne y el esfuerzo

de nuestro pueblo ascendiente

nos han robado el amor;

lo han convertido en moneda

cuanto tiene juan?

déjame ver si te quiero

las murallas del miedo

levanta el monstruo entre pueblos

entre hermanos que se acuchillan

mientras la máquina explota, mata

mata y envenena

envenena nuestras venas

con licor   .

con heroína, con hamburguesas

con hot dogs, y aspirinas

y desodorantes

que esconden el aroma

de los cuerpos que sufren

gozan, duelen

y crecen con el amor

en las venas, en la carne, en los huesos

raza, raza, raza, raza

el amor nos pertenece

nuestras canciones lo cantan

nuestra carne lo demanda

we love you carnal, carnala

jefe y jefa los queremos

el carnalismo nos une y

el amor hacia nuestros hermanos y hermanas

nos hace un pueblo ascendiente

GUERRA: PODER: PAZ-
UNA CARTA A TIZOC

es importante clarificar

    que el poder y la paz

se oponen el uno al otro solo en las naciones

    que alimentan

    sus estómagos

con una economía de guerra

    que compite por los mercados

en la tierra traficando

    usando y propagando

el narcótico del alto

    y creciente nivel de vida

de los pocos en el mundo adictos a la guerra.

para los muchos...

    el carnalismo es necesario, la guerra es obsoleta:

y la paz es otra fuente de poder

    con violencia

le falta la claridad y el coraje

    para actuar

a través de veredas de creación

cuando hay paz

en nuestro corazón, la única lucha que lidear

es en contra de nuestros enemigos naturales:

    el miedo

        la claridad

            el poder

    y la vejez

actos violentos para derrotar estos

    enemigos naturales

de la especie humana

son actos suicidas

    cometidos

    en contra de uno mismo,

    en contra de la raza

actos no violentos

    tienen sus raíces en

nuestra tierna relación

    con el coraje

y nuestro respeto por

    el ciclo natural

de capullos florecientes

al marchitar de las flores al explotar de las semillas

de nuevo la paz extrae poder

de la vida y el sacrificio colectivo del ser

de los muchos oprimidos

    la guerra está fundada y es mantenida

por la muerte y la explotación individual del ser

para beneficio de los pocos opresores

el poder y la paz

pueden jalar juntos

y perpetuar la familia

de la raza humana -

nuestra

madretierra,

padresol,

y todos sus hijos vivientes

nuestros carnales y carnalas

la hermana hormiga, la hermana abeja

el hermano lobo

y el hermano árbol

la hermana flor

y el hermano maíz.

WHO ARE WE?...
SOMOS AZTLÁN:
A LETTER TO
"EL JEFE CORKY"

a dog walks waggling

   its tail, proud

its chest out

   and its head high

another comes

   and fights him under the moon

tears all possible skin

   off each other

the first

   wins

and walks away in darkness

   having established power

through violent struggle, the other runs

   a month later

the dog no longer walks waggling

   its tail

another dog tears him

   ragged and fearful, the night before

with its tail between

   its legs, defeated, runs himself in darkness again

defeated by the people's

first natural enemy:

   fear

the fear that all

    of us once face

before our christian ignorance

we see unknown evils/the devil or communism

    unknown feelings/the body or violence

    unknown thoughts/the mind or guilt

    unknown threats/death or god

    unknown pictures/dreams or nightmares

and we run, we run

we run, when we could walk, and see clearly;

without violence,

    we could walk

the path we all must walk:

    the path of peace, the path of peace

for those who want the power

    to impart life, knowledge, nourishment, and health.

weed out the paths of war

of those who exploit the power

    to bring death

and genocide

against one's self, the human race, suicide

    through governments

built with firepower

    and violent

military dictatorships.

in this country

       the united states

of (i beg your pardon)

           northamerikkka, yankeeland

general george washington

     became its first

commander general of the armed forces

     and its first

military dictator, president

     today, thursday

september ten

     san diego a.m.

before dawn break

     two thirds of every

u.s. federal tax dollar

     are spent

     on the military/for defense

we do not believe in suicide,

     or homicide,

     or genocide, or biocide

we do not wish to walk the deadly path

     of fear while living.

we shall walk the path of courage

       and disciplined,

defeat, the people's enemy, fear with nonviolently

rooted power, our weapon justicia

to: establish peace,

restore the earth,

and respect the sun;

peace, earth and sun: peace, earth and sun

can bring our

liberation from

ignorance, war, hunger, disease,

and military dictatorships

be they white

or black,

their violence must end

with our culture, our heart, and our peace.

YA ESTUFAS

espumado con atoles de nubes

        el cielo colorado

witnessed a dusk

        of murals

           painted

in the spirit

        of liberación nacional

in the spirit

        of the fallen

brown dry leaves

        of autumn

las cananas en

        la tarde

aparecieron and

        thousands

of bullets

        turned

    to flowers,

kissed la raza's heart

        and many Mexicans

cried "ya estufas

        viva la revolución"

5☉LAR GR☉WTH

aranda's calavera

died silenced

      with chains

        trying to breath peace

and his birth as

      a Tolteca

    took its shape

in wood

in lacerated agony

      and painful

chips and chissled

      birth

again guillermo

      flowered

and sung his

      heart's poemas

to the moon

      of his inspiration

and the solace

      of his

solar growth

TORTILLA HOST

a circle round

      the sun again

the pace of our pueblo

      del sol la vuelta

ha dado otra

      vez, otra nube

aparece en la eterna

      tarde

tarde nunca llega el

      sol, al tiempo

explota y su piel se cubre

      de llagas

se limpia, se prende

      se apaga su sed

in the sacrifice

      que regresa

      que se lanza

a la vida solar

      y la tierra materna

espera fecunda

      fecunda

      fecunda la raza del sol

as mountains

breathe el aliento

de Ehecatl pues

Tlaloc en su rabia mojada

has rinsed

of dust and of clouds

la luz

morning, morning breaks

in la playa mojada

and the ardent flesh

quenches the pain

as the pebbles of sand

in ayunas a star

brings salt to our lips

moistened dawn

otro año carnal, carnala se nos llega

nos pierde, nos pasa

y nos deja arrugada la piel

longing

longing for the freedom

that hides

in the shadow

we tear at our tripas

in hate bitting

our lips for its freshened caress

time, otro año carnal, carnala
el sententa con uno se
                viste y nos deja
memorias y luces
                perdidas en la
oscuridad lápida
                del pasado/la muerte
now pasa y la vida
                invita otra copa
did you see los espejos
                los reflejos del año
pasado de Aztlán
        el primero
        el del grito nacido en el pecho
now llorando
now playing, now singing
                but crawling on fours
chavalito: la nación es joven
                apenas si el pueblo
se junta
                the nation has brought
to its nipple many
                muchos que maman
la chichi del movimiento sin

ser·hijos del sol y la luna

la luna los niega

bastardos sin padre y

sin madre vagando en

la noche de miedos

hay que velar: the movement is young

hay que velar el amanecer

dawn is breaking

and the sunset builds

castles in wet afternoons

enero, enero

el primero se rompen los jarros

clay is sacrificed

al año

del sol encuerado

many sour fruits

will flavor el año

del sol uno y setenta

más su pueblo must face

opression

colonization

by the yankee empire

opressed con hambre

con ganas, con sed

the colonized with chains

en el corazón

the razared

of

Amerindia,

our continent,

clamors

as

liberation and unification

pierce our senses

smell/breathe

touch the nipples

of cornfield mountains

and drums/move the movement

dream a life

live a dream

cast off nightmares

cast off fears

eat a plate of frijoles

and rejoice in

cebolla

let tortillas be host to your heart

ETERNAL TRIPAS ✳

the átomos of

our tripas, raza

can fly

to the fathersun

on motherearth's tortillas

gather your stones carnales

get your canicas back

back, back to the flowing

water causeways

of Tenochtitlan

back to the tears of Tlaloc's agony

to the stillness of our sun

Ollintonatiuh, back to Aztlán

our son of movement

el retorno a la luz

entre la noche y el día

el grito de dolores

despierta

la

energía

que no se mueve

en el rojosol del movimiento

MAR DE SANGRES . ⁘

writing words
                to crack open empty silence,
and find nopales independientes
                con tunas carnes rojas
vivas.   many a drop of rain
                has fallen;
over inflamed cheeks and
        dripping nosed chicanitos
                cough in los barrios
of dust. as the comal on our heart
        warms our blood and we play
                with our children round, and round
chicano man.

                hear the screaming, crying
wailing winds.

        all autumn leaves are flying
over the banquetas - junto a los yonkes
                de califas, arizona
                        new mexico, colorado
nevada, utah, texas, kansas, illinois.
                junto a los yonkes
in every barrio there is raza, raza

among the canneries/beyond the tracks
      some racist places hide the raza
            of the land in dark stench corners
of smog and howling humans
      freeze
      in the fields of profit
to the yankee clocked in christian time
      shrouded with green money
    and shiny guns of frozen death
sabes que, carnal, carnala
      no me cae
    esta fuerza del yanki
      basada en nuestra muerte
      no me cae
la independencia
      nace en el corazón de
los individuos
      para florecer entre los pueblos
    bajo el sol
      en la tierra we walk
      en la tierra we speak
      en la tierra we love
      en la tierra we die
and find birth breaking
      in the mornings

chicano independence must dawn

        before economic progress

and the welfare of pockets

           is filled; uncle sam's

have anchored profit

        in the country's heart of coin

economic independence

        the movement of the pueblos

against dictatorships of money

        before our sun: Ollintonatiuh

comes to the end of its cycle

        the strong in heart shall rise,

survive, and bear the burden of

        the weakened yankee minds

they refused to accept death

        and

        froze

        their

        bodies

        cold

        mechanic flesh

        of efficient inmortality

        in ice; these shall

           melt

           before

           our moving sun

now dawning

carnalismo...

dentro de nuestro corazón

blood flows at an even pace

and all violent rivers

return to the calm

of deep oceanos

social change in uncle sam's organization

band-aids wounds

y niega la sangre derramada

en guerras

nunca

declaradas con

viet-nam, laos, cambodia

con el pueblo del rojosol naciente

y manda raza

con pistolas y muerte

then peace corps band-aid

rushingly the scars of war

with good-willed uncle sam's

big brothers to be watched raping

bronze sisters.

in the stillness of our heart

dedication can be found

to la causa

    la causa de toda esclavitud

    y muerte

con tierra y libertad

      ha de acabar/the burden

        the burden is ours

          raza

          raza

          raza

          raza

black, white, red

          raza

          raza

          raza

in our mixed blood

          all

          have

          come

          to

          be

          carnales

en el mar de sangres.

WINDLESS VENAS

guitarras tardes
  soleadas mañanas
como rios corren
  los pensamientos
and the sea of theories
  splashes on the rocks of
established white wash shores;
  drowning brotherhood and sisterhood
once held in blood
  the tide of placas viene
tirando mordidas y pedradas miradas
wacha las aguas del rio
wacha las aguas del mar
  todas calmadas regresan
toda violencia apaga su sed
  con los espejos del mar
  de colores sangres
derramadas
  las venas: our cause ways
are windless at sea.

GROW STRONG

entre colorados cielos

the blazing redness of

a sun

now sinking

our flesh in the waters

our veins are refreshed

in our struggle

to be free to breathe

las caidas y ascensos de nuestro padresol

our father bleeds; smog clouds

prevent him

from touching our skins.

fathersun touch us with your radiant breath

give us warmth

motherearth weeps for your caresses

lost today in poisoned clouds

fathersun! come!

brighten our faces

into gleaming bronce!

carve pride on our cheekbones!

give wisdom to our heart!

let us, raza, determine our path

let us, raza, conquer fear amongst us

and in our imagesun

our flesh grow strong...

our bones grow strong,

our blood grow strong!

> carnal! carnala!

our heart grow strong...!

RAZA

SOLAR CLIFFS ☼

entre rocas de niebla justicia
            nuestro padre sereno
                        se baña en la tarde.
se retira el abuelo solar en el cielo;
            and the winds, in their maritime breathing,
moisten nostrils of salted
                        caresses of freshness
to the stillness of time calaveras
            las olas...
            las olas...
marea, marea as our solar tradition
            cracks open the waters
the earth and sky in a fire flown sundown
well painted by sun reddened clouds
            oh! our father, be still!
stay with us on the path with a heart
            burning, stay, burning
            splashing, stay, splashing
            in wisdom

DANZA LEONINA

zipping through concrete telarañas

metallic ants turn to centipedes

and bright lights darken the ojos

of one who see the neon

and towers of smoking oil refineries

of los angeles muertos

muertos en la tarde de agosto

the maiz was trampled by dogs

and many birds took flight

in the maze, the crying

cursing winds of northern icelands

in the summer

walk again on earth

and sing of peace and carnalismo

de raíces terrenales

proviniente de fecundo vientre

man stands and walks again

on earth

to listen with plantas descalzas

to the murmuring caress of

motherearth's latidos

she gave us birth in blood

and for the sun we have sacrificed

hasta los huesos tostados

en los desiertos de la incandescencia

                    del señor padresol
we have marched
                    migrated, walked the distance
of our lives in lonely stroll
                    below the moongloom of the night
as cherry headed armored ants wail
                    in the night of fire and smoke
splashing mud on sidewalk and walls
                    rushing to the hunt belly clubbed
gas masked, shot gun panting breaths
                    se chorrean de gusto de muerte
                    se chorrean de muerte de gusto
retiring at dawn to the beer canned existence
                    of idiot box stares, waiting
waiting for the prowling sunset of
                    another asphalt telaraña ride
riding over brotherhood
                    danza
                    riding over sisterhood
                    danza
riding over justice
                    danza
riding over peace

danza de plantas encueradas

danza de raza

danza de barro

danza de espíritu

danza de bronce

danza, danza, danza, danza

AQUÍ NOMÁS

as the lápida of our flesh

all things once born on earth

be gone... aquí no más

someday, someplace

motherearth devours her children

and so she will

me

and

you

and

we, sin embargo

where are we? donde estamos?

aquí nomás carnales y carnalas

aquí nomás

en la tierra

que como a sus hijos nos de chichi

nos dá maíz

quí nomás

encontramos un sueño

our lives are the images we mirror

while children

on earth

we need not dream

        suicide, homicide

        genocide or biocide

our hearts must find our spot

        our place, our body

        our family, our tribe

        our nation and our motherearth

will welcome the return of her children

to her womb and our flesh

and her flesh shall be our dormant life

        again around our fathersun

        again

        again

        again

        again

aquí nomás en la tierra

        en la tierra aquí nomás

LEVÁNTATE Y RÍE

in the mud
    butterflies found birth
flying to the sun
    from the stillness of time calaveras
the eyes of all wrinkles
    come on to nopales
shedding their flesh in tears
    to the sun while on earth
las flores escuchan
    el canto del hombre
que penetra el silencio
como un niño que llora
    y que todo a la boca se mete
la nación se atraganta de miedos
y llora frustrada pues sus piernas
    le tiran al suelo
    y sus marchas no escucho ni el
    cielo, ni el sol
más su llanto penetra la tierra
y la madre le escucha
    "Aztlán, Aztlán
levántate hija, camina, hijo

yerge tu espina y busca tu sol

       yo te doy maíz

no comas el veneno de yankee

       mastica, mastica

       tu maíz

hazme el amor, digiere mi leche

       escucha el

         latir

       de mi pecho, escucha

         descalzo

que tu carne es mi carne

       eres tierra

         hija, Aztlán

       eres tierra

que tu sangre es la sangre del sol

       eres sol

        levántate y ríe

       que en tu vida

de espinas

       la tuna se dá

levántate y come

       mama mi chichi, olvida el dolor

si tropiezas y caes

       levántate

mama mi chichi, olvida el dolor

crece, grow

mama mi chichi, olvida el dolor

vuela, mariposa

vuela, you have crawled

enough

as worn

vuela, mariposa

vuela, you have slaved

enough

in chains

vuela, mariposa

vuela you have toiled

enough

with earth

vuela, mariposa

vuela, you will meet

the bearded redsun once again

DAWN EYE COSMOS

what if we wanted to climb

to the mountains

and seek lakes of serpents

and eagles hunting

in the carrizales

caña por suerte encontrásemos

y maíz plantásemos

que la tierra fuera libre

y el sol brought flowers

in the songs of our hearts

what if we lived

with the tierra

treasuring the cracks in the sky

of dawn eyed cosmos

or sunset retiradas del señor/señora

do we want to go

and blow up a building

or can we change

the place of many

pueblos heart

marching

through the calles

cantando about nuestra

nación

ofreciendo la vida
            a cambio de armonía
cantando de colores
            sarapes mañanas
"buenos días carnal, carnala;
            el sol amaneció con
nosotros
            y ha de partir en paz"
            the borders of all territories
            cannot last forever
"razared, you don't have to fix
                  the fence"
            and uncle sam
                  need

                  not

                  kill

                  for

                  markets

                  and

                  cheap

                  labor

                  pools
we
            don't have to slave or consume war's flesh
the thunder clouds
            of our hearts
                        bring rain
to the smog of war:

and charcos

de agua temprana

flicker with the

face of Quetzalcoatl

and the surrounding

eyes of night

let Ehecatl/señor del viento

change the course

of our nubes

we need not

kill sam or sacrifice his heart

sam is suicidal

sam is killing himself

we need not

spill his blood

but then

we don't need to buy his death, or eat

his chemical replacement for organic life,

or sell ourselves

to his war of hate and fear and profit.

we can say

buenos días!

señor y señora

del cosmos ojos de amanecer

buenos días, corazón ! late!

late corazón

late y canta

tu canción

               sing your pain
                   and pleasure
                        heart, give us
     your love unto death
               give us
     your death unto love
     sing of the mirror
          and the face
     sing of the labyrinth
          and the heart
     sing of the dawn
          and the dusk
     sing of la razaroja
          and the cause, canta, corazón, canta

RAZA